THE BIBLE

Too Tall, Too Small

Luke 19:1-10

by Mary Manz Simon

Illustrated by Dennis Jones

SPIRIT PRESS

Read and Learn the Bible
LEVEL 1

This edition published in 2004 by Spirit Press, an imprint of Dalmatian Press, LLC.

ISBN: 1-40371-156-9
Printed in Canada
13798-1004

04 05 06 07 QSR 10 9 8 7 6 5 4 3 2 1

This Book Belongs to

Name

Date

To the Adult:

Early readers need two kinds of reading. They need to be read to, and they need to do their own reading. The *Read and Learn the Bible* series helps you to encourage your child with both kinds.

For example, your child might read this book as you sit together. Listen attentively. Assist gently, if needed. Encourage, be patient, and be very positive about your child's efforts.

Then perhaps you'd like to share the selected Bible story in an easy-to-understand translation or paraphrase.

Using both types of reading gives your child a chance to develop new skills and pride in reading. You share and support your child's excitement.

As a mother and a teacher, I anticipate the joy your child will feel in saying, "Hear me read a Bible story!"

Mary Manz Simon

And he ran before, and climbed up
into a sycamore tree to see him:
for he was to pass that way.
LUKE 19:4

See the people.

The people want to see Jesus.

"I want to see Jesus,"
said Zacchaeus.
"I want to see Jesus, too."

"The people are too tall,"
said Zacchaeus.
"I am too small."

“I will climb up, up to see,”
said Zacchaeus.
“Jesus will be close to me.”

“The people are too tall.
The animals are too tall.
I am too small,”
said Zacchaeus.

“I will climb up, up to see,”
said Zacchaeus.
“Jesus will be close to me.”

See the people.
See the animals.
See Zacchaeus.

"The people are too tall.
The animals are too tall.
The trees are too tall.
I am too small," said Zacchaeus.

“I want to see Jesus.
I want to see Jesus, too.”

The people are tall.
The animals are tall.
The trees are tall.

"The trees are tall,"
said Zacchaeus.
"Wow!"

"I will climb the tree,"
said Zacchaeus.
"I will climb the tall, tall tree."

"I will climb up, up to see,"
said Zacchaeus.
"Jesus will be close to me."

“I see Jesus.
I see Jesus come.
Jesus will see me,”
said Zacchaeus.

“Zacchaeus,” said Jesus.
“Zacchaeus, come see Me.
Come close to Me.”

“Wow!” said Zacchaeus.

Read and Learn

24 words that tell the Bible story.

WORD LIST

I	see	tall	climb
to	the	will	small
am	too	come	Jesus
up	are	said	people
be	wow	tree(s)	animals
me	want	close	Zacchaeus

About the Author

Mary Manz Simon holds a doctoral degree in education with a specialty in early childhood education. She has taught at levels from preschool through post-graduate. Dr. Simon is the bestselling author of more than 40 children's books, including *Little Visits with Jesus*. She and her husband, the Reverend Henry A. Simon, are the parents of three children.